CACTI

CACTI

CHARTWELL
BOOKS, INC.

Published by Chartwell Books
A Division of Book Sales Inc.
114 Northfield Avenue
Edison, New Jersey 08837
USA

ISBN 0-7858-0978-3

This book is produced by
Quantum Books Ltd
6 Blundell Street
London N7 9BH

Project Manager: Rebecca Kingsley
Project Editor: Judith Millidge
Design/Editorial: David Manson
Andy McColm, Maggie Manson

The material in this publication previously appeared in
Illustrated Encyclopedia of Cacti

QUMSPCI
Set in Futura
Reproduced in Singapore by Eray Scan
Printed in Singapore by Star Standard Industries (Pte) Ltd

Contents

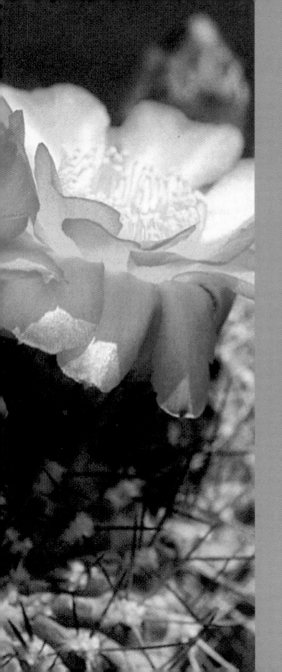

BEAUTIFUL CACTI

Cacti have many rare and beautiful features, developed during a long and slow evolutionary process. One of their principal characteristics is the ability to adapt to harsh conditions which would cause most other plant groups to perish quickly.

The Living World of Cacti

With over 150 genera and several thousand species the cactus family (Cactaceae) is a very large one. The need to survive, under even the harshest conditions, probably causes the intriguing shapes — some even bordering on grotesque— which cacti display.

CACTI STRUCTURE

The shapes and sizes of cacti are almost infinite. Their common feature is a fleshy inbuilt structure that is apparent in either their stem, leaves or roots. This structure enables them to store moisture and helps protect them against environmental conditions and changes.

CACTI HABITAT

The Cactaceae are distinguished from other succulent plant families by having a growing point called an areole. Not all cacti are from arid or semi-arid regions. Many are jungle or rainforest plants, some even living in the trees, such as *Epiphyllum Ackermanii.*

Left. Epiphyllum Akermanii, *a tree-dwelling cactus from the Brazilian rainforest.*

Above. Superb examples of cacti in mixed planting arrangement behind glass.

INDOOR CACTI

The number of cacti suitable for indoor cultivation is enormous. Comparatively few are mentioned in these pages, but those described are representative of hosts of others that will add brightness and interest to your home. Obviously some are not so easy to grow as others. Those from equatorial regions demand more warmth than those from tropical areas, so care is needed if the two are to be kept together.

MIXED CACTI

If mixed plantings of cacti are desired, be careful to select species which have similar needs in terms of soil type, temperature light and general cultivation. This is particularly important when planting bowl gardens, where plants are closely confined.

Never plant cacti in a bottle garden. It may seem an attractive idea initially, but the micro-climate in a bottle is far too extreme and cacti would not survive.

Caring for Cacti

There are a number of general guidelines to cultivation that will assist you and ensure success when raising and caring for individual species and varieties, as well as mixed plantings.

LIGHT

Different species of cacti will need varying amounts of light, depending on their original habitat. Desert species require the brightest and sunniest positions possible or they become mis-shapen and are unlikely to flower. Jungle and rainforest cacti dislike direct sunlight. However, a reasonable amount of light is essential for photosynthesis.

TEMPERATURE

One of the all-important factors in the cultivation of cacti is temperature. There may be widely variable demands depending on the requirements of the individual plants in your collection. During the summer months, normal room temperature is usually adequate for plants used for home decor. Specific temperatures are noted in the directory section (see p.16).

Left. Ferocactus latispinus, *a popular easily grown cactus from Central Mexico.*

Above. Echinocereus viereckii, *a desert cactus from Tamaulipas in Mexico.*

WATERING

Success in growing cacti is dependent upon correct watering more than any other factor. Lack of water can lead to dehydration while overwatering can lead to black rot. In the wild cacti are subject to seasonal rainstorms followed by periods of drought. When watering follow this natural pattern. Soak well, then allow to dry out before watering again. The best time to water is early morning or late evening — never in the heat of the day, as this can lead to scorching.

FEEDING

Proper feeding is also important. Without it, growth will become retarded and, if flowers develop at all, they will be of poor quality. Feeding is best combined with watering, the fertilizer being applied in diluted form every 3–5 weeks during the growing season. Choose a comprehensive fertilizer—one with essential trace elements of iron, magnesium, iron, copper, cobalt, manganese and molybdenum together with the standard nitrogen, potassium and potash.

Locating your Cacti

For those of you who are unfamiliar with the names of cacti and may have some plants that you would like to try to identify, the guide on these pages may help. It gives a breakdown of the main groups by shape.

GLOBULAR

Few or no spines
Astrophytum, 19–20
Echinocereus, 24–6
Turbinicarpus, 62

With fine spines
Escobaria, 30
Gymnocalycium, 33–5
Mammillaria, 38–42

Short straight spines
Echinocereus, 24–6
Neoporteria, 45
Sclerocactus, 57

Flat or prominent tubercules
Ariocarpus, 18
Echinocereus, 24–6
Turbinicarpus, 62

Woolly or spiny crown
Matucana, 43
Notocactus, 46
Parodia, 50–52
Weingartia, 63

Prominent spines
Echinocactus, 23
Echinocereus, 24–6
Echinofossulocactus, 27
Echinopsis, 28
Ferocactus, 31
Lobivia, 37

With prominent cephalium
Melocactus, 44

CLIMBING

Hylocereus, 36

PENDENT

Segmented pendent
Schlumbergera, 56

Angular pendent
Aporophyllum, 18
Borzicactus, 20
Heliocereus, 36
Selenicereus, 58

LEAF-LIKE

Broadly leaf-like
Epicactus, 29

COLUMNAR

Erect or semi-prostrate
Borzicactus, 20
Echinocereus, 24–6

Bushy
Mammillaria, 38–42
Opuntia, 47–8

Spiny
Borzicactus,20
Trichocereus, 61

Short columnar
Astrophytum, 19
Borzicactus, 20
Echinocereus, 23–6
Lobivia, 37
Mammillaria, 38–42

PADDED/JOINTED

Opuntia, 47–8

CLUSTERING

Cushion-like clusters
Mammillaria, 38–42
Rebutia, 54–5
Sulcorebutia, 59

Group-forming
Echinocereus, 24–6
Escobaria, 30
Ferocactus, 31
Gymnocalycium, 33–5

Sparse clusters
Chaemolobivia, 21
Matucana, 43
Sulcorebutia, 59

SPRAWLING/TRAILING

Firm sprawling stems
Echinocereus, 23–6

Slender, strong spines
Trichocereus, 61

THROUGHOUT THE DIRECTORY

In the directory pages of this book (see p.16), the icons in the green boxes denote the shape of each individual cacti.

B E A U T I F U L   C A C T I

Pests and Diseases

All plants are vulnerable to attack by insect pests and cacti are no exception. Although humans can also do quite a bit of damage through neglect or too much care.

INSECTS AND BUGS

The most common pests associated with cacti are mealy bugs, root mealy bugs, red spider mites, scale insects, sciarid flies and their larvae, aphids. Growing conditions can prevent some infestation. For example, red spider mites attack if the atmosphere is too dry and hot; regular spraying with water is recommended as a deterrent.

HUMAN OVERKILL

Overwatering and insufficient drainage can lead to a bacterial infection known as black rot, when the base of the plant turns black. Such a condition must be treated promptly or it will prove fatal. Cut away the infected area and treat with sulphur powder. Reddish spots on the plant are signs of overwatering in the full heat of day causing scorching.

How to Use the Book

The information in the directory section of this book is arranged to supply the reader with a snapshot of each species. A number of icons have been used which are explained below.

SHAPE (see also p.12)

Globular   Columnar   Climbing

Padded/   Pendent   Leaf-like
jointed

Clustering   Sprawling

FLOWERING PERIOD

Mid-winter   Late winter to   Mid-spring
           early spring

Late spring to   Mid-summer   Late summer to
early summer   early autumn

Mid-autumn   Late autumn to
           early winter

FLOWERING TIME

 Day flowering

 Night flowering

LIGHT

 Good but indirect light

 Partial shade

 Full shade

 Direct sunlight

---

Left. Rebutia senilis, displaying a profusion of carmine red flowers.

CACTI
SPECIES

This book is planned to provide ease of use, even by a complete cactus novice. In the illustrated directory of the Cactaceae that follows, you will find examples of over 90 individual cacti. They are arranged in generic groups, and the species are identified alphabetically, according to their botanical nomenclature.

ARIOCARPUS KOTSCHOUBEYANUS

Plants are up to 3in in diameter with close-set tubercles, flat on upper surface and dark green, with a woolly furrow. Flowers grow from the center of the plant. Water in moderation late spring and early summer; keep dry in winter.

Syn *Roseocactus koyschoubeyanus, Anhalonium koyschoubeyanus.*
Origin Mexico.
Plant size 2³/₄in diameter.
Flower size 1¹/₂in long; 2in wide.
Flower color Purplish or pink.
Minimum temp. 50°F.
Location Very bright light.

ARIOCARPUS TRIGONUS

The plants have many semi-erect, grayish-green tubercles at the base. Aeroles are spineless. The flowers arise from the axils of the tubercles and are yellowish, diurnal. Needs a gritty, but enriched compost and no water in winter.

Syn *Anhalonium trigonum.*
Origin Mexico.
Plant size 4–6in diameter.
Flower size 2in wide.
Flower color Yellowish.
Minimum temp. 56°F.
Location Bright and sunny.

ASTROPHYTUM ASTERIAS

A globular, solitary species, slightly flat on the top with up to ten flat ribs, with straight grooves between and, white, conspicuous spineless areoles set lengthwise on the ribs. The flowers are diurnal in summer, slightly reddish in the throat.

Syn *Echinocereus asterias.*
Origin Mexico.
Plant size 4in diameter.
Flower size 1¼in long; 1½in wide.
Flower color Yellow.
Minimum temp. 45°F.
Location Sunny.

ASTROPHYTUM CAPRICORNE

Plants are globular, becoming oval with about nine acute ribs, deeply grooved between with brownish areoles and dotted with many whitish scales. Flowers are diurnal, growing from areoles near to the top.

Syn *Echinocereus capricornis; Maierocactus capricornis.*
Origin. Northern Mexico.
Plant size 4in diameter.
Flower size 2¾in wide.
Flower color Yellowish to brownish-black.
Minimum temp. 56°F.
Location Bright and sunny.

A S T R O P H Y T U M

BORZICACTUS ROEZLII

Columnar, grayish-green, with seven to fourteen ribs notched above each areole. Areoles are yellowish with nine to fourteen brownish radial spines and one grayish central. The tips of the stems are covered with tufts of bristles through which tubular flowers appear in summer.

Syn *Seticereus roezlii.*
Origin Northern Peru.
Plant size 3–6ft high.
Flower size 2³/₄in long
Flower color Red.
Minimum temp. 50°F.
Location Bright light is essential.

BORZICACTUS SAMAIPATANUS

An erect, later pendent plant with bright green stems and 14–16 ribs. The areoles are brownish and bear 13–22 slender yellowish-brown spines. Day flowering in summer, the flowers are tubular and curved.

Syn *Bolivicereus samaipatanus;*
Cleistocactus samaipatanus.
Origin Bolivia.
Stem size 5ft long.
Flower size 2¹/₂in long.
Flower color Deep red with paler edges.
Minimum temp. 50°F.
Location Sunny position.

CHAMAELOBIVIA 'FIRECHIEF'

A colorful hybrid of *Lobivia x Echinopsis x Chamaecereus (Lobivia) silvestrii* developed by Harry Johnson of the USA. One of the most startling cultivars yet produced. Night flowering species needing partial shade.

Syn None.
Origin USA.
Plant size 4in.
Flower size 2in.
Flower color Orange.
Minimum temp. 50°F.
Location Partial shade.

CHAMAELOBIVIA 'JOANNE'

A brilliantly colored cultivar of *Lobivia silvestri* and *Lobivia jajoiana*. The 'peanut'-like stems of the first parent are more stunted, but the vivid flower clearly depicts the other parent, *L. jajoiana*. Flowering in mid-summer, it is diurnal and needs good light.

Syn None.
Origin USA.
Plant size 3¹/₄ in.
Flower size 2in.
Flower color Orangy red.
Minimum temp. 50°F.
Location Good light.

CORYPHANTHA/CLEISTOCACTUS

CLEISTOCACTUS STRAUSII

A branching, columnar plant with stems 39in or more high, up to 3¹/₄in thick, totally covered with silvery white spines. The light green stems have 25 ribs; the areoles have 30 or more snow-white bristly spines and four longer pale yellowish spines.

Syn *Pilocereus strausii.*
Origin Bolivia.
Plant size 39in high.
Flower size 3¹/₂in long.
Flower color Carmine red.
Minimum temp. 50°F.
Location Full sun.

CORYPHANTHA OTTONIS

A short cylindrical plant, it is dark green, with very thick grooved tubercles and woolly axils. Spines are yellowish; there are eight or more radials, and one or more centrals. Flowers appear by day in summer.

Syn *Mammillaria golziana.*
Origin Mexico.
Plant size 4³/₄in diameter.
Flower size 2in wide.
Flower color White or pale yellow.
Minimum temp. 50°F.
Location Good light.

22

ECHINOCACTUS GRUSONII

A large globose plant over 1m (39in) high, and pale green in color. It has 25–35 sharply defined ribs with areoles carrying spines of eight to ten radials and three to five centrals. Flowers occur only on mature plants, from the crown.

Syn *'Golden Barrel'* or *'Mother-in-Law's Cushion'*.
Origin Mexico.
Plant size Over 39in high.
Flower size 2¹/₂ in long.
Flower color Bright yellow.
Minimum temp. 50°F.
Location Bright sun.

ECHINOCACTUS HORIZONTHALONIUS

A glaucous-green globular plant with seven to thirteen ribs often spirally arranged. Areoles bear six to nine radial spines and one central; the radials are sometimes curved. The flowers appear in summer and are diurnal.

Syn None.
Origin USA, Mexico.
Plant size 10 in high.
Flower size 2³/₄ in long.
Flower color Rose or pink.
Minimum temp. 59°F.
Location Full sun.

ECHINOCEREUS ADUSTUS

A short, cylindrical, rarely caespitose species, and dark green. It has 13–15 ribs, and closely set areoles, with 16–20 widely spreading radials and one central. Flowers are diurnal appearing in early summer.

Syn *Echinocereus caespitosus var. adustus.*
Origin Northern Mexico.
Plant size 2¹/₂in high.
Flower size 1¹/₂in long.
Flower color Pinkish purple.
Minimum temp. 45°F.
Location Bright light.

ECHINOCEREUS KNIPPELLIANUS

A very dark green globular, almost oval plant, with five to six rounded ribs divided by broad furrows. The areoles are very small with one to three spines, which quickly fall. Flowers appear in spring and again in early summer.

Syn None.
Origin Mexico.
Plant size 2in diameter.
Flower size 1¹/₂in long.
Flower color Pink.
Minimum temp. 50°F.
Location Sunny.

ECHINOCEREUS MERKERI

An erect or semi-prostrate species with stems of grayish green, with eight to nine rounded ribs with prominent tubercles. The areoles are grayish white set with six to nine white radial spines and one or two centrals.

Syn None.
Origin Northern Mexico.
Plant size 12in high.
Flower size 2³/₄in long.
Flower color Purplish red.
Minimum temp. 50°F.
Location Good light.

ECHINOCEREUS PECTINATUS

The 'type' of a most variable species. Plants are either globose or short and cylindrical. The 22–30 radial spines are whitish or pinkish, arranged like a comb, and there are about three very short centrals. Flowers are diurnal.

Syn None.
Origin USA, Mexico.
Plant size 4–6in diameter.
Flower size 2in wide.
Flower color Pale pinkish lavender with a white throat.
Minimum temp. 50°F.
Location Sunny.

ECHINOCEREUS

ECHINOCEREUS SUBINERMIS

The stems are globular becoming elongated and clustering occasionally. Dull green, they have five to nine prominent ribs with narrow furrows between. Small woolly areoles bear three to eight radial spines and one central, later becoming spineless.

Syn None.
Origin Mexico.
Plant size 6in long.
Flower size 3^1/$_4$in long and wide.
Flower color Yellow.
Minimum temp. 50°F.
Location Sunny.

ECHINOCEREUS VIERECKII

A semi-prostrate species with long, pale green stems, with seven to nine tuberculate ribs. Areoles bear whitish or yellowish spines: seven to eleven radials and three to five centrals. The flowers are diurnal.

Syn None.
Origin Mexico.
Plant size 8in high.
Flower size 4^1/$_2$in wide.
Flower color Deep pink or magenta.
Minimum temp. 50°F.
Location Bright.

ECHINOFOSSULOCACTUS PENTACANTHUS

Grayish-green globular plants with 30–40 wavy-edged ribs bearing very few areoles. These have five grayish-brown spines, the upper ones to 5cm (2in) long, the lower to 1/3 in. Flowering diurnally in spring, the flowers are 3/4 in long.

Syn *Stenocactus pentacanthus.*
Origin Central Mexico.
Plant size 3 1/4 in diameter.
Flower size 3/4 in long.
Flower color Whitish with a pale purple mid-stripe.
Minimum temp. 50°F.
Location Full sun.

ECHINOFOSSULOCACTUS PHYLLACANTHUS

A dark bluish-green globular plant with 30–35 thin, wavy edged ribs bearing areoles. The spines are red, passing to brown. There are two to seven in all, the upper three are flat, the others are slender and spreading. Day flowering in late spring.

Syn *Anhalonium trigonum.*
Origin Mexico.
Plant size 3 1/4 in diameter.
Flower size 2in wide.
Flower color Yellowish white.
Minimum temp. 50°F.
Location Sunny.

ECHINOPSIS KERMESINA

Currently considered a variety of *E.mammillosa Gürke*. The plants are globular and a rich green, having 15–23 ribs with areoles bearing reddish-yellow radial spines and four to six darker centrals. Day flowering in mid-summer.

Syn None.
Origin Argentina.
Plant size 6in diameter.
Flower size 7¹/₄in long.
Flower color Carmine red.
Minimum temp. 56°F.
Location Bright light is essential.

ECHINOPSIS OXYGONA

Globular stems become cylindrical, and offsetting from around the sides. There are 13–15 ribs with large, short woolly areoles. The pale-brownish spines consist of 13–15 radials and two to seven centrals.

Syn None.
Origin Southern Brazil, Argentina, Uruguay.
Plant size 10in diameter.
Flower size 10in long; 4³/₄in wide.
Flower color Pale pink internally, reddish externally.
Minimum temp. 50°F.
Location Full sun.

EPICACTUS 'ACHIEVEMENT'

One of the earliest yellow-flowering cultivars to be developed in the UK, the product of *Echinopsis aurea* and *Epiphyllum crenatum*. Flowers have slightly frilled petals, and need filtered light, and an acid, porous compost.

Syn None.
Origin UK.
Plant size 14in.
Flower size 5$^1/_2$in wide.
Flower color Yellow.
Minimum temp. 50°F.
Location Filtered light.

EPICACTUS 'BALLYSHAVEL'

This is a very colorful cultivar originated in the USA. A richly colored flower, it appears in late spring. The flowers last up to three days, opening in mid-morning, and partially closing near dusk. Needs a slightly shaded position.

Syn None.
Origin USA.
Plant size 14in.
Flower size 4$^3/_4$in wide.
Flower color Deep lilac and purple blend.
Minimum temp. 50°F.
Location Slightly shaded position.

ESCOBARIA HESTERI

A small, globular, clustering species, it often forms clumps up to 12in in diameter in the wild. The stems are dull green with conical tubercles. There are 14–16 pale brownish-yellow radial spines, but no centrals. Flowering in summer, it is diurnal.

Syn *Coryphantha hesteri.*
Origin USA.
Plant size 12in high.
Flower size 1in long and wide.
Flower color Bright purple.
Minimum temp. 56°F.
Location Bright light.

ESCOBARIA MINIMA

The dark-green stems are more or less oval, solitary or clustering. The tubercles are conical, and the grooves bare. There are 13–15 radial spines and three centrals: these spines are pinkish, becoming gray.

Syn *Coryphantha minima;*
Coryphantha nellieae.
Origin USA.
Plant size 1in high.
Flower size ½in wide, ¾in long.
Flower color Rose pink.
Minimum temp. 50°F.
Location Slight shade.

FEROCACTUS DIGUETII

A large species eventually reaching to
13ft tall and more or less
globular as a young plant. The stems
are dark green with about 34 ribs
when fully grown, the areoles bearing
six to seven reddish-yellow radial
spines and one central, slightly curved.

Syn *Echinocactus diguetii.*
Origin Mexico.
Plant size 13ft high.
Flower size 2³/₄ in long.
Flower color Yellow inner petals, and
reddish-brown outer ones.
Minimum temp. 50°F.
Location Sunny.

FEROCACTUS EMORYI

A large globular, later cylindrical, plant
with 30–32 ribs. The large oval brown
woolly areoles, bear five to eight white
or reddish radial spines and one flat,
hooked central. The flowers are centred
towards the crown of the plant.

Syn *Ferocactus covillei; Echinocactus
emoryi.*
Origin Mexico, USA.
Plant size 5ft high
Flower size 2³/₄ in)long.
Flower color Red with yellow-tipped
petals, or entirely yellow.
Minimum temp. 50°F.
Location Full sun.

FEROCACTUS LATISPINUS

A broadly globular species of grayish-green, with a slightly flattened top. The 15–23 ribs are rather notched with large gray areoles carrying six to twelve pale radial spines, and four reddish centrals, the lower one hooked with a flattened surface.

Syn *Cactus latispinus.*
Origin Mexico.
Plant size 10–16in wide.
Flower size 2in wide.
Flower color Whitish, yellowish or purplish.
Minimum temp. 50°F.
Location Sunny position.

FEROCACTUS SETISPINUS

A globular, later elongating, species. Dark green it offsets when old. There are 13 ribs, notched and often wavy, with areoles. The spines are white or brown, consisting of six to fifteen radial spines and one to three centrals, hooked.

Syn *Hamatocactus setispinus.*
Origin Northern Mexico.
Plant size 6in high.
Flower size $3/4$ in.
Flower color Yellow with a red center.
Minimum temp. 50°F.
Location Full sun.

GYMNOCALYCIUM CASTELLANOSII

A solitary, globular species, velvety
bluish green in color with 10–12 broad
ribs. The white woolly areoles bear five
to seven dark-tipped whitish radial
spines with sometimes one
central. Flowers are white flushed with
pink and day flowering.

Syn None.
Origin Northern Argentina.
Plant size 6in high.
Flower size 1³/₄ in wide.
Flower color White flushed with
pink.
Minimum temp. 50°F.
Location Slight shade.

GYMNOCALYCIUM LEEANUM

A bluish-green, rather flattened globular
plant with up to 15 ribs divided into
more or less six-sided tubercles. There
are up to 11 radial spines and
occasionally one central. Flowers
bloom in early summer and are diurnal.

Syn None.
Origin Argentina, Uruguay.
Plant size 3in diameter.
Flower size 2¹/₂ in long and wide.
Flower color Yellowish white.
Minimum temp. 50°F.
Location Slight shade.

GYMNOCALYCIUM PLATENSE

Stems are green to bluish-green, with 12–14 ribs divided into obtuse warts. There is a prominent chin below each of the gray woolly areoles, which have five to seven radial spines. There are no centrals.

Syn None.
Origin Argentina.
Plant size 4in high.
Flower size 2in wide.
Flower color White with a reddish throat, outer segments bluish-green externally.
Minimum temp. 50°F.
Location Very light shade.

GYMNOCALYCIUM QUEHLIANUM

This is one of several varieties which differ in certain features from the species. The grayish-green, globular plant has about 15 prominent ribs and about seven widely spreading pale-brownish radial spines. The flowers are diurnal, appearing in mid-summer.

Syn Rose Plaid cactus.
Origin Argentina.
Plant size 5in wide.
Flower size 2in.
Flower color Lilac-pink.
Minimum temp. 50°F.
Location Slight shade.

GYMNOCALYCIUM RIOJENSE

A brownish-green or dull-greenish globular plant with about 15 broad ribs. The areoles bear five to seven pale brownish-yellow spines. The flowers are diurnal and appear in summer.

Syn None.
Origin Argentina.
Plant size 3¼ in high.
Flower size 1¾ in wide.
Flower color Reddish sepals and whitish petals with a reddish mid-stripe.
Minimum temp. 50°F.
Location Light shade.

GYMNOCALYCIUM SPEGAZZINII

This solitary, globular species is very popular. Bluish green or grayish green to brownish in color. There are 10–15 ribs and the areoles bear reddish-brown to grayish spines, five to seven curved radials and occasionally one central.

Syn None.
Origin Argentina.
Plant size 7 in diameter.
Flower size 2¾ in long.
Flower color White or pinkish white.
Minimum temp. 50°F.
Location Slight shade.

GYMNOCALYCIUM

HYLOCEREUS OCAMPONIS

A forest climbing plant, glaucous green with slight wavy margins, and usually three-angled. The areoles are brownish-red with five to eight yellowish spines. Flowering in mid-summer, the blooms are nocturnal, with wide inner segments and narrower outer segments.

Syn *Cereus ocamponis.*
Origin Mexico.
Plant size 10ft long.
Flower size 12in long.
Flower color Pure white inner and pale yellowish green outer.
Minimum temp. 59°F.
Location Partial shade.

HYLOCEREUS UNDATUS

A widely cultivated species with stems divided into joints and freely branching. Climbs by its ariel roots. Areoles are set at intervals along the 'winged' margins with a few short, dark spines.

Syn *Cereus undatus; Hylocereus tricostatus.*
Origin Probably West Indies.
Plant size 4–6in diameter.
Flower size 11¾in long.
Flower color White inner segments, outer ones yellowish-green.
Minimum temp. 56°F.
Location Bright position.

LOBIVIA BACKBERGII

The pale green plant is solitary or offsetting, globular or oval, with about 15 spirally notched ribs. Areoles have three to seven brownish, spreading radial spines, often curved or hooked; there are no centrals.

Syn *Echinopsis backbergii.*
Origin Bolivia.
Plant size 2 in diameter.
Flower size 2¹/₄ in long.
Flower color Carmine red.
Minimum temp. 45°F.
Location Very bright position.

LOBIVIA SILVESTRII

The popular Peanut Cactus is a dwarf species with pale-green stems, branching and offsetting freely. The seven to ten ribs bear whitish, bristly spines. Flowers appear in early summer, bright scarlet, and diurnal.

Syn *Chamaecerus silvestrii.*
Origin Argentina.
Plant size 6in.
Flower size 2in long.
Flower color Bright scarlet.
Minimum temp. 45°F.
Location Slight shade.

MAMMILLARIA BARBATA

Globular plants, often clustering. Each stem is apple-green, with numerous, wide-spreading, slender spines consisting of 50–60 white radials, often with brownish tips, and one or two hooked centrals. A summer, day-flowering species.

Syn None.
Origin Mexico.
Plant size 4–6in diameter.
Flower size $3/4$ in long.
Flower color Pale straw-colored.
Minimum temp. 45°F.
Location Sunny position.

MAMMILLARIA BLOSSFELDIANA

A globular, solitary species. It is dark green with close-set areoles bearing 15–20 yellowish, black-tipped radial spines and three to four black centrals, one being hooked. Flowers are diurnal and appear in early summer.

Syn *Mammillaria shurliana.*
Origin Mexico.
Plant size $1^{1}/2$ in diameter.
Flower size $1^{1}/4$ in long; $3/4$ in wide.
Flower color Pale pinkish with a deep carmine-red center stripe.
Minimum temp. 56°F.
Location Bright position.

LOBIVIA BACKBERGII

The pale green plant is solitary or offsetting, globular or oval, with about 15 spirally notched ribs. Areoles have three to seven brownish, spreading radial spines, often curved or hooked; there are no centrals.

Syn *Echinopsis backbergii.*
Origin Bolivia.
Plant size 2 in diameter.
Flower size 2$^1/_4$ in long.
Flower color Carmine red.
Minimum temp. 45°F.
Location Very bright position.

LOBIVIA SILVESTRII

The popular Peanut Cactus is a dwarf species with pale-green stems, branching and offsetting freely. The seven to ten ribs bear whitish, bristly spines. Flowers appear in early summer, bright scarlet, and diurnal.

Syn *Chamaecerus silvestrii.*
Origin Argentina.
Plant size 6in.
Flower size 2in long.
Flower color Bright scarlet.
Minimum temp. 45°F.
Location Slight shade.

MAMMILLARIA BARBATA

Globular plants, often clustering. Each stem is apple-green, with numerous, wide-spreading, slender spines consisting of 50–60 white radials, often with brownish tips, and one or two hooked centrals. A summer, day-flowering species.

Syn None.
Origin Mexico.
Plant size 4–6in diameter.
Flower size $3/4$ in long.
Flower color Pale straw-colored.
Minimum temp. 45°F.
Location Sunny position.

MAMMILLARIA BLOSSFELDIANA

A globular, solitary species. It is dark green with close-set areoles bearing 15–20 yellowish, black-tipped radial spines and three to four black centrals, one being hooked. Flowers are diurnal and appear in early summer.

Syn *Mammillaria shurliana.*
Origin Mexico.
Plant size $1^{1}/2$ in diameter.
Flower size $1^{1}/4$ in long; $3/4$ in wide.
Flower color Pale pinkish with a deep carmine-red center stripe.
Minimum temp. 56°F.
Location Bright position.

MAMMILLARIA CHIONOCEPHALA

A solitary, globular plant, later developing offsets to form clusters. The bluish-green stems have four-edged tubercles and thick white woolly axils. There are 22–24 white radial spines, and two to six white or brownish centrals, tipped black and hooked.

Syn *Mammillaria ritterana.*
Origin Mexico.
Plant size 4³/₄ in high and wide.
Flower size ¹/₂ in wide.
Flower color White to pale pink, with a reddish median line on the petals.
Minimum temp. 50°F.
Location Bright and sunny.

MAMMILLARIA ELEGANS

Synonymous with *M. haageana.* A solitary plant, offsetting in maturity. Globular to cylindrical stems, with a woolly, spiny crown. Close-set tubercles with whitish woolly areoles bearing 25–30 white radial spines and one or two brown-tipped white centrals.

Syn *Mammillaria dealbata.*
Origin Mexico.
Plant size 4–6in high; 4¹/₄ in wide.
Flower size 2in wide.
Flower color Carmine red.
Minimum temp. 50°F.
Location Full sun.

MAMMILLARIA HUMBOLDTII

A solitary, rarely clustering species with more or less globular stems. The tubercles are very small with bristly, woolly axils. Areoles have up to 80 or more white radial spines, but no centrals. Summer flowering, it is diurnal.

Syn None.
Origin Mexico.
Plant size 2in diameter.
Flower size 1 1/4 in long and wide.
Flower color Purplish red.
Minimum temp. 50°F.
Location Sunny.

MAMMILLARIA LENTA

A small globular plant, sometimes clustering. Each stem has slender tubercles, and axils with short wool and often one bristle. Areoles bear 30–40 clear-white to pale-yellowish radial spines, but no centrals. The flowers appear in summer and are diurnal.

Syn None.
Origin Mexico.
Plant size 1/2 – 3/4 in diameter.
Flower size 3/4 in wide.
Flower color White with a pale-purple median line to the petals.
Minimum temp. 50°F.
Location Bright position.

MAMMILLARIA MICROCARPA

The pale-green plants are cylindrical, and usually clustering, with conical tubercles and bare axils. The areoles carry 18–30 whitish radial spines and one to three reddish-brown centrals. Summer flowering, the plant is diurnal.

Syn None.
Origin Mexico, USA.
Plant size 6in high.
Flower size 1in long; 2¹⁄₄ in wide.
Flower color Rose-pink.
Minimum temp. 50°F.
Location Full sun.

MAMMILLARIA SEMPERVIVI

A globular plant which 'reluctantly' offsets. The stems are dark green, with slender pyramidal tubercles and dense wool in the axils. Areoles bear three to seven white radial spines, and two, rarely four, reddish or yellowish centrals.

Syn Mammillaria pseudocrucigera.
Origin Mexico.
Plant size 3¹⁄₄ in diameter.
Flower size 1¹⁄₂ in wide.
Flower color Whitish or yellowish pink, with a reddish median stripe in the petals.
Minimum temp. 50°F.
Location Sunny.

MAMMILLARIA TAYLORIORUM

The stem is globular, solitary or clustering. It has conical tubercles, and the axils are woolly when young, then sparse with one or two bristles. There are about 12 brownish-tipped white radial spines and two or five centrals similar to the radials. Summer flowering and diurnal.

Syn None.
Origin Mexico.
Plant size 10in high.
Flower size 5/8 in wide.
Flower color Pinkish with white.
Minimum temp. 50°F.
Location Full sun.

MAMMILLARIA ZEILMANNIANA

A well-known, popular species. The dark-green globular stems readily cluster, with somewhat oval cylindrical tubercles and bare axils. The 15–18 radial spines are white, almost hair-like; there are four reddish-brown central spines, one hooked.

Syn None.
Origin Mexico.
Plant size 2 1/2 in high.
Flower size 3/4 in long.
Flower color Reddish violet, pinkish or white.
Minimum temp. 50°F.
Location Sunny position.

MATUCANA KRAHNII

A grayish-green, more or less globular, clustering species, with about 18 ribs divided into prominent, broadly conical tubercles. The areoles are white with dark-brownish spines, about eight radials and one to four centrals. The flowers are slightly zygomorphic.

Syn *Borzicatus krahnii.*
Origin Peru.
Plant size Not known.
Flower size 2³/₄ in wide.
Flower color Deep reddish lilac.
Minimum temp. 65°F.
Location Bright and sunny.

MATUCANA OREODOXA

Globular, bright grayish-green plants, sometimes offsetting to form clusters. It has seven to twelve bumpy ribs and very small areoles bear four to twelve yellowish-brown spines which later turn gray.

Syn *Eomatucana oreodoxa;*
Borziacactus oreodoxa.
Origin Peru.
Plant size 4in diameter.
Flower size 1¹/₂–2¹/₂ in long.
Flower color Reddish orange with a paler throat.
Minimum temp. 56°F.
Location Bright position.

MELOCACTUS MATANZANUS

A globular, pale-green plant with eight to nine straight ribs. The spines are brownish white or grayish, with seven to eight radials and one central. The cephalium is densely covered with reddish-brown bristles. Diurnal after midday in the summer.

Syn None.
Origin Cuba.
Plant size 3¹/₂ in high.
Flower size ⁵/₈ in wide.
Flower color Pink.
Minimum temp. 61°F.
Location Full sun.

MELOCACTUS OAXACENSIS

A dull-green more or less globular plant. It has 11–15 deeply furrowed ribs with areoles. There are eight to twelve reddish-brown radial spines and one central. The cephalium is ³/₄ in–2¹/₄ in high and has dense brown bristles and a whitish woolly top.

Syn None.
Origin Mexico.
Plant size 4–6in diameter.
Flower size ⁵/₈ in long.
Flower color Pink.
Minimum temp. 61°F.
Location Bright sun.

NEOPORTERIA PLANICEPS

Also known as *N. Laniceps*. A more or less globular species with 13–17 bumpy ribs. The areoles are white and bear 50 hair-like spines including, usually, two brownish centrals. The flowers are diurnal in late summer.

Syn None.
Origin Northern Chile.
Plant size 8in high.
Flower size 1¼in long.
Flower color Carmine red.
Minimum temp. 56°F.
Location Good light.

NEOPORTERIA OCCULTA

Small globular plants, yellowish-brown to almost black in color, with eight to ten prominently tuberculate ribs. The areoles are whitish, bearing six to ten radial spines and one central; all tend to fall with age. Flowers are diurnal in summer.

Syn *Neochilenia occulta*.
Origin Chile.
Plant size ½–1in wide.
Flower size ¾in wide.
Flower color Pale yellow.
Minimum temp. 50°F.
Location Bright position.

NOTOCACTUS POLYCANTHUS

Dark-green, globular plants with 17 notched ribs. The areoles are whitish and bear six to eight whitish radial spines with usually one central. Early flowering and diurnal.

Syn *Wiginsia polyacantha.*
Origin Southern Brazil.
Plant size 4 in wide.
Flower size 3/4 in wide.
Flower color Canary yellow with prominent reddish stigma lobes.
Minimum temp. 50°F.
Location Sunny position.

NOTOCACTUS UEBLMANNIANUS

A dark-green globular species, some-what flattened on the upper surface. It has 12–16 prominent thick ribs and large, white areoles with six to eight grayish white radial spines. Mid-summer flowering, it is diurnal.

Syn None.
Origin Brazil.
Plant size 7 in wide.
Flower size 2 in long and wide.
Flower color Glossy red.
Minimum temp. 50°F.
Location Bright light.

OPUNTIA BRACHYCLADA

A low growing, spreading plant with small grayish-green joints. They bear many small brownish areoles with brown glochids which are spineless. Flowers are cup-shaped and appear by day, in summer. A choice, quite rare plant.

Syn *Opuntia brachyclada.*
Origin USA.
Joint size 2–3^1/$_4$ in long.
Flower size 3^1/$_4$ in wide.
Flower color Deep red
Minimum temp. 45°F.
Location Full sun.

OPUNTIA DISCOLOR

A semi-prostrate plant with very dark green joints, and almost cylindrical in shape. It has dark brown areoles with brown glochids. There are usually two or three grayish-brown spines. The plant blooms by day in summer.

Syn None.
Origin Argentina.
Joint size 2–6 in long.
Flower size 1^1/$_4$ in wide.
Flower color Bright yellow.
Minimum temp. 50°F.
Location Good, bright light.

OPUNTIA ORBICULATA

A tall, shrubby plant up to 6ft high with oval or roundish joints and glaucous or pale bluish green in color. The areoles are grayish, with reddish-yellow glochids, becoming grayish-white. Numerous whitish hairs are very apparent on the surface of the joints.

Syn *Opuntia crinifera*.
Origin Northern Mexico.
Plant size 6ft high.
Flower size 4in wide.
Flower color Yellow.
Minimum temp. 45°F.
Location Sunny position.

OPUNTIA PULCHELLA

A clump-forming species arising from a glochid-covered tuber. The joints are mostly cylindrical or clavate and covered with low tubercles. The areoles have yellow glochids and whitish or grayish spines of which eight to fifteen are radials and there is one central.

Syn None.
Origin USA.
Plant size 4 in high.
Flower size 2in wide.
Flower color Purple to rose.
Minimum temp. 50°F.
Location Sunny position.

OREOCEREUS CELSIANUS var FOSSULATUS

Stems are erect and columnar, branching from the base with nine to fourteen ribs. The areoles bear honey-yellow spines and many hairs. The flowers are red or brownish-red and appear by day, in summer.

Syn *Oreocereus fossulatus.*
Origin Peru, Bolivia.
Plant size 5ft.
Flower size 3¹/₂in long.
Flower color Red or brownish red.
Minimum temp. 50°F.
Location Bright sunshine.

OREOCEREUS DOELZIANUS

The olive-green stems have nine or more ribs. Gray silky areoles bear 10–16 radial spines and four centrals. Flowers appear by day in summer from the dense, white, woolly and bristly cephalium.

Syn *Morawetzia doelziana; Morawetzia sericata.*
Origin Central Peru.
Stem size 1¹/₂–3in thick.
Flower size 4in long.
Flower color Carmine with a bluish suffusion on the inner petals.
Minimum temp. 50°F.
Location Bright sun.

OREOCEREUS

PARODIA CLAVICEPS

A dark-green, more or less cylindrical, club-shaped plant with around 26 ribs. The areoles are whitish, carrying many somewhat drooping spines.
Mid-summer flowering and diurnal.

Syn *Wiginsia corynodes.*
Origin Paraguay, Brazil.
Plant size 20 in high.
Flower size 2 in wide.
Flower color Sulphur yellow.
Minimum temp. 50°F.
Location Bright position.

PARODIA HASELBERGII

A grayish-green, globular plant with 30 or more ribs and the woolly crown set at an angle. The white areoles bear 20 or more yellowish-white radial spines, and three to five centrals.
Summer flowering and diurnal.

Syn *Notocactus haselbergii;*
Brasilicactus haselbergii.
Origin Brazil.
Plant size 8 in wide.
Flower size 5/8 in long.
Flower color Yellowish red.
Minimum temp. 50°F.
Location Bright light.

PARODIA HORSTII

A globular plant with a spiny, white woolly crown. It has 12–16 ribs, and the areoles bear 10–15 white or slightly brownish radial spines and one to four, brown centrals. The plant is summer flowering by day.

Syn *Notocactus horstii.*
Origin Brazil.
Plant size 5¹/₂ in wide.
Flower size 1¹/₄ in long.
Flower color Orangy-red to vermillion.
Minimum temp. 56°F.
Location Bright light.

PARODIA LENINGHAUSII

A globose later columnar species with the crown set at an angle. The small, white areoles bear about 15 pale yellow radial spines and three to four deeper yellow centrals. Day flowering in mid-summer.

Syn *Eriocactus leninghausii;*
Notocactus leninghausii.
Origin Southern Brazil.
Plant size 39 in high.
Flower size 2 in wide.
Flower color Bright yellow.
Minimum temp. 50°F.
Location Sunny position.

PARODIA MALAYANA var RUBRIFLORA

A bright-green globular plant with 24 or more slightly spiralled ribs. The whitish areoles bear over 20 grayish-brown, darker tipped radial spines and two to three or more fine centrals.

Syn None.
Origin Argentina.
Plant size 2¹/₂ in wide.
Flower size 1¹/₂ in wide.
Flower color Bright red, funnel- shaped.
Minimum temp. 50°F.
Location Bright light is essential.

PARODIA MUTABILIS

A high-altitude, globular species. It is glaucous green with a white woolly crown and ribs arranged in spirals. The white woolly crown areoles bear about 50 whitish radial spines and most usually four centrals. Day flowering in summer.

Syn None.
Origin Argentina.
Plant size 8 in wide.
Flower size 2 in wide.
Flower color Bright golden yellow.
Minimum temp. 50°F.
Location Very bright light.

PILOSOCEREUS GLAUCOCHROUS

An erect or semi-erect, bluish-green columnar species. It has five to nine deep, notched ribs and white hairy areoles. These bear nine to twelve pale brownish-yellow radial spines and three to four similarly colored centrals. Summer flowering in the daytime.

Syn *Cephalocereus glaucochrous.*
Origin Brazil.
Plant size 13ft high.
Flower size 2$^{1}/_{2}$in long.
Flower color Pale pink or whitish inner petals and greenish-red outer segments.
Minimum temp. 56°F.
Location Full sun.

PILOSOCEREUS SCHOEBELII

An erect columnar species, developing branches like a candelabra. The stems and branches are pale blue, with 12 ribs and creamy-white areoles. Spines are pale-brownish, later grayish black, 16–20 radial spines and four centrals. The pseudocephalium consists of a few tufts of whitish wool.

Syn None.
Origin Brazil.
Plant size 13ft high.
Flower size 2$^{1}/_{2}$in wide.
Flower color Whitish-green.
Minimum temp. 56°F.
Location Full sun.

REBUTIA ALBIFLORA

A globular, clustering plant, the bright-green individual stems are often slightly elongated. It has 14–16 spirally arranged ribs and areoles with up to 15 fine whitish radial spines and about five centrals. Day flowering.

Syn *Aylostera albiflora.*
Origin Bolivia.
Plant size 3¼ in long.
Flower size 1 in long.
Flower color White with a pale pinkish mid-stripe.
Minimum temp. 45°F.
Location Bright light.

REBUTIA HELIOSA

A small gray-greenish, slightly flattened globular to short cylindrical plant, which offsets freely. It has 35–40 ribs arranged spirally, with low tubercles. The brown-felt areoles have 24–26 comb-like spines, but no centrals. Day flowering in summer.

Syn None.
Origin Bolivia.
Plant size ¾ in high.
Flower size 1½ in wide.
Flower color Orange or reddish.
Minimum temp. 50°F.
Location Full sun.

REBUTIA NARVAECENSIS

A clustering species with grayish-green, somewhat globular stems. It has about 18–22 spirally arranged ribs set with low tubercles. The creamy-brown felted areoles bear white or brown spines, 20–30 radials, and up to six hardly distinguishable centrals.

Syn *Aylostera narvaecensis.*
Origin Bolivia.
Plant size 1¹/₄ in high.
Flower size 1¹/₂ in wide.
Flower color Pale rose pink.
Minimum temp. 50°F.
Location Slight shade.

REBUTIA SENILIS

A deep-green, flattened-globular species. It has about 18 spirally arranged ribs divided into tubercles. Areoles are white and bear about 25 yellowish-white fine spines, often matted together. On rare occasions an interesting cristate form develops, coupled with a profusion of flowers.

Syn None.
Origin Argentina.
Plant size 3¹/₄ in high.
Flower size 1¹/₄ in wide.
Flower color Carmine red.
Minimum temp. 50°F.
Location Bright position.

SCHLUMBERGERA x BUCKLEYI

This is the popular Christmas Cactus. The stems are composed of flat, oval joints arranged like links. The flowers are zygomorphic, appearing in late autumn and winter from the areoles at the tips of the uppermost segments.

Syn *Schlumbergera x bridgesii.*
Origin Hybrid origin.
Plant size 1ft wide.
Flower size 3in long.
Flower color Bright red.
Minimum temp. 56°F.
Location Filtered light.

SCHLUMBERGERA ORSSICHIANA

A fascinating epiphyte with pendant stems of flattened segments or joints. The margins have two to three prominent teeth with areoles set in the angles. Daytime flowers are produced from the tips of terminal joints in late winter and also in late summer.

Syn None.
Origin Brazil.
Stem size 2$^{1}/_{2}$in long.
Flower size 2in long and wide.
Flower color White with reddish margins to the petals.
Minimum temp. 50°F.
Location Full sun.

SCLEROCACTUS PAPYRACANTHUS

A short cylindrical globose plant, either solitary or grouping. It has eight to thirteen ribs with prominent tubercles and areoles bearing five to nine whitish radial spines, and three to four flat, curving centrals. The flowers are diurnal, in summer, and appear from the crown.

Syn *Echinocactus papyracanthus;*
Toumeya papyracantha.
Origin USA.
Plant size 3¹/₄ in high.
Flower size ³/₄ in long.
Flower color Whitish.
Minimum temp. 50°F.
Location Sunny position.

SCLEROCACTUS PARVIFLORUS

A cylindrical plant, but usually remaining globular during the earlier years. The stem is bluish-green and it has 13 ribs with whitish areoles set on prominent tubercles. There are nine to fifteen grayish radial spines and one to three centrals. The flowers are diurnal and appear in mid-summer.

Syn None.
Origin USA.
Plant size 18 in high.
Flower size ³/₄ in wide.
Flower color Pinkish-purple.
Minimum temp. 50°F.
Location Sunny, bright position.

SELENICEREUS

SELENICEREUS GRANDIFLORUS

A variable species with trailing or climb
ing stems. It has five to eight ribs and
pale-yellowish woolly areoles bearing
seven to eleven yellow spines which
become gray. Flowering at night in
summer, the blooms are fragrant, with
broad petals and spreading sepals.

Syn *Cereus grandiflorus.*
Origin West Indies, Mexico.
Stem size 17ft long.
Flower size 12in long; 6in wide.
Flower color Pale-yellowish-brown.
Minimum temp. 59°F.
Location Semi-shade.

SELENICEREUS INNESII

A trailing species, it has six ribs and
woolly areoles with one or two thick
and three to seven slender pale-brown
spines. It is unique within the
Cactaceae as some plants bear only
male flowers, others only female,
whilst on some plants there are normal
flowers.

Syn None.
Origin St Vincent (West Indies).
Stem size 6¹/₂ft long.
Flower size 2in long.
Flower color Pinkish white.
Minimum temp. 59°F.
Location Filtered light.

58

SULCOREBUTIA MENESESII

A dark grayish-green clump-forming species. Each globular stem has 14–18 spiralling ribs. The white woolly areoles bear 10–15 brown-tipped whitish radial spines. Flowers are diurnal, appearing in summer.

Syn None.
Origin Bolivia.
Stem size 1¹/₂ in high.
Flower size 1¹/₂ in long.
Flower color Pale to bright yellow.
Minimum temp. 50°F.
Location Bright light.

SULCOREBUTIA RAUSCHII

A clustering plant composed of small blackish-green or purplish-green stems with up to 16 spiralling ribs. The areoles are almost bare, rarely one or two centrals. Day flowering in early to mid-summer.

Syn None.
Origin Bolivia.
Stem size ³/₄ in long.
Flower size 1¹/₄ in long.
Flower color Magenta pink or purple.
Minimum temp. 50°F.
Location Full sun.

THELOCACTUS HASTIFER

A pale grayish-green globular, solitary species, only rarely offsetting. It has 18–20 tuberculate ribs and white woolly areoles when young. The spines are white, 20–25 radials and four centrals. Summer flowering and diurnal.

Syn *Ferocactus hastifer.*
Origin Mexico.
Plant size 6 in high.
Flower size 3^1/$_2$ in high.
Flower color Pinkish with a violet-pinkish center to the petals.
Minimum temp. 50°F.
Location Full sun.

THELOCACTUS SCHWARZII

Bluish-green globular plants with about 13 ribs. The areoles are whitish, bearing 13–14 reddish, yellowish-tipped radial spines, but no centrals. Day flowering in summer.

Syn *Thelocactus macrochele var. schwarzii.*
Origin Mexico.
Plant size 2^1/$_2$ in high.
Flower size 3^1/$_2$ in wide.
Flower color Pale reddish purple.
Minimum temp. 50°F.
Location Full sun.

TRICHOCEREUS HUASCHA

A dark-green, much-branching species with 12–18 ribs. The whitish-brown areoles are very close-set and bear nine to eleven brownish radial spines, and one or two centrals. Mid-summer flowering and diurnal.

Syn *Helianthocereus huascha; Echinopsis huascha.*
Origin Argentina.
Stem size 20–35in high.
Flower size 4in long.
Flower color Golden yellow.
Minimum temp. 50°F.
Location Sunny position.

TRICHOCEREUS SPACHIANUS

Tall, dark-green columnar plants, freely branching from the base, with 10–15 ribs. The areoles are yellowish becoming gray, and bear yellowish-brown spines, 8–10 radials and one, often two or three, centrals. Night flowering in mid-summer.

Syn *Echinopsis spachianus.*
Origin Western Argentina.
Plant size 6ft high.
Flower size 8in long; 6in wide.
Flower color White inner petals and greenish outer segments.
Minimum temp. 50°F.
Location Bright position.

TURBINICARPUS PSEUDOMACROCHELE

Dull-green, miniature plants with ribs divided into small tubercles. White terminal areoles bear six to eight adpressed spines. Diurnal flowers in summer. Keep dry in winter.

Syn *Strombocactus pseudomacrochele: Neolloydia pseudomacrochele.*
Origin Mexico.
Head size 1¹/₂ in wide.
Flower size 1¹/₄ in wide.
Flower color Pale pinkish with a pale-reddish median stripe.
Minimum temp. 50°F.
Location Full sun.

TURBINICARPUS VALDEZIANUS

An attractive sub-globose miniature plant, it has a long subterranean stem, with only the rounded top exposed. The bluish-green ribs are divided into tubercles arranged spirally, and are four angled. There are numerous white and hair-like spines.

Syn *Pelecyphora valdeziana; Normanbok valdeziana.*
Origin Mexico.
Stem size ³/₄–1³/₄ in wide.
Flower size ³/₄ in long.
Flower color Reddish purple.
Minimum temp. 56°F.
Location Sunny position.

WEINGARTIA MULTISPINA

A pale-green, semi-globular plant, covered with large prominent conical tubercles. The areoles have whitish-brown wool. The spines are yellowish with 25–30 radials and 25–30 centrals. Flowering in summer, the plant is diurnal.

Syn None.
Origin Bolivia.
Plant size 5^1/$_2$ in wide.
Flower size ^{3}/$_4$ in long.
Flower color Bright yellow.
Minimum temp. 50°F.
Location Bright light.

WEINGARTIA NEOCUMMINGII

A most variable species; the bright to dark-green stems are semi-globular, with about 16–18 tuberculate ribs. Areoles bear 16–20 yellowish, brown-tipped radial spines and about six more centrally placed spines. Day flowering in summer.

Syn None.
Origin Bolivia.
Stem size 8 in high.
Flower size 1 in long.
Flower color Orange, shading to a yellow throat.
Minimum temp. 50°F.
Location Bright position.

W E I N G A R T I A